T0061947

SOUL OF AMSTERDAM

A GUIDE TO THE 30 BEST EXPERIENCES

WRITTEN BY BENOIT ZANTE
PHOTOS BY PAULINE WALZAK
ILLUSTRATED BY PHILIPPINE LUGOL

JONGLEZ PUBLISHING

Travel guides

'SOME TOURISTS THINK AMSTERDAM IS A CITY OF SIN, BUT IN TRUTH IT IS A CITY OF FREEDOM'

JOHN GREEN, AMERICAN AUTHOR

Why do we love Amsterdam?

People still associate Amsterdam with its coffee shops, flower market and red-light district. Millions of tourists from all over the world visit every year, attracted by – among other things! – the city's spirit of freedom. Yet Amsterdam is so much more than this handful of clichés.

Crisscrossed by canals, it's a dynamic, open city which you can explore on foot, by bicycle or even by boat. With its relatively small size, low population density and many parks, its residents enjoy a quality of life that is rare for a city of its size. Above all, Amsterdam refuses to rest on its laurels, instead constantly demonstrating its ability to reinvent itself and remain at the cutting edge of modernity. The whole city is a symbol of this: in the centre, centuries-old houses, often leaning at odd angles, exist side-by-side with some of today's most innovative companies and brands.

This guide is not meant to give you an exhaustive view of the city; plenty of other books do that. Rather, it aims to offer a glimpse of its diversity through a selection of experiences that capture the soul of Amsterdam – and that will make you want to spend more than just a weekend there!

WHAT YOU WON'T FIND
IN THIS GUIDE

- information about the red-light district
- a metro map
- a guide to the coffee shops

WHAT YOU WILL FIND
IN THIS GUIDE

- a rooftop where you can dangle your feet in the water
- places to take a dip
- the brewery where you can have a beer in the shadow
  of a windmill
- markets where you can go for a stroll and discover local specialitie
- how to sleep amidst the canals

SYMBOLS USED IN
'SOUL OF AMSTERDAM'

Less
than €20

€20
to €50

More
than €100

Reservation
is recommended

So
Ámsterdam

Go there by bike

30 EXPERIENCES

EAT HERRING
LIKE THE DUTCH

Fishing boats abandoned the port of Amsterdam long ago – nowadays, you have to cycle a few dozen kilometres to Volendam or Marken to see them. But the city has not renounced its past as a port.

At the various fish stalls in the city centre, you can try raw herring, freshly caught (*verse haring*) or salted (*zure haring*), depending on the season. Some people eat it with onions and gherkins on bread (*broodje haring*), but the traditional way is to let it slide straight down your throat ...

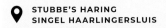

STUBBE'S HARING
SINGEL HAARLINGERSLUIS

On the bridge between the
Singel and Haarlemmerstraat

HARING & ZO
NIEUWEZIJDS VOORBURGWAL 200

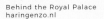

Behind the Royal Palace
haringenzo.nl

HOW TO EAT
HERRING
DUTCH STYLE?

There are two ways

let it slide
straight down
your throat

with onions
and gherkins
on bread

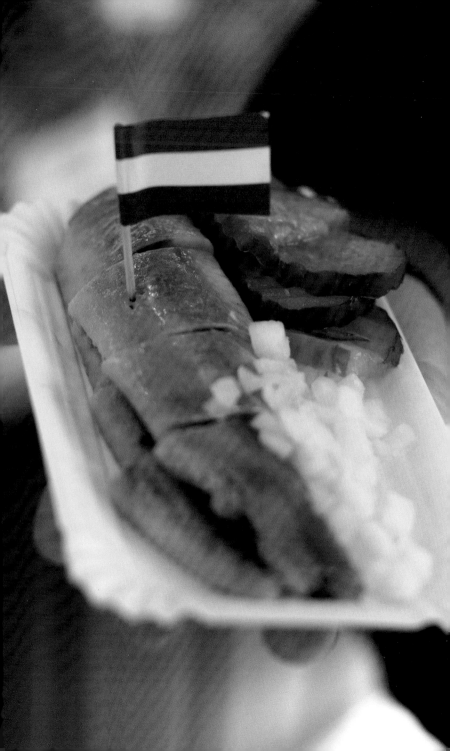

COCKTAILS
ON A ROOFTOP,
FEET IN THE WATER

After a day roaming the streets on foot or by bike or exploring the Rijksmuseum, it's time to get a sense of perspective. A few metres from Dam Square, hidden on the roof of the W Hotel, a long swimming pool awaits you: the perfect place to sip a cocktail while dangling your feet in the water and waiting for the sun to set.

**W LOUNGE
SPUISTRAAT 175**

wloungeamsterdam.com

ROAM AROUND
THE ALLOTMENT GARDENS

The *volkstuinen* (allotment or community gardens) have been a city institution since the late 19th century: some have a small house, others are simple vegetable gardens, but each has its own personality. Today, applicants sometimes wait ten years before they get the opportunity to rent a garden in one of the city's 29 *volkstuinparks* ... But, starting in early spring, you can go for a wander along the paths in some of them, including the central gardens nestled in the heart of Westerpark.

 SLOTERDIJKERMEER
SLOTERDIJKERWEG 20

275 allotments
sloterdijkermeer.nl/15v1

 NUT EN GENOEGEN
SLOTERDIJKERWEG 22

375 allotments
nutengenoegen.amsterdam
instagram.com/nutengenoegen

AN *APPELTAART* ALONG THE CANAL

The apple pies from this café in the Jordaan quarter are considered the best in the city. Their secret? Generous chunks of apple, crust as tender as it is crispy and a cloud of whipped cream … It's no wonder that, the moment the sun comes out, the smell of baking pies attracts a quickly growing queue of visitors and locals outside Winkel43 … especially on market days at the nearby Noordermarkt (organic food on Saturday, antiques on Monday).

To save time, get your pie to take away and find a spot a bit further along the canal to savour it.

WINKEL43
NOORDERMARKT 43

winkel43.nl/en

A BUBBLE
OF CALM

You'll find it hard to believe you're still in the middle of the hustle and bustle of Amsterdam the moment you walk through the doors of this townhouse. Built on the ruins of a former theatre, this bubble of calm incorporates a bakery from 1797 that has been transformed into a Michelin-starred restaurant. With comfortable rooms, duplex suites under the roof and large windows overlooking the canal or inner garden, this hotel might well be the best place to stay in Amsterdam.

THE DYLAN
KEIZERSGRACHT 384

dylanamsterdam.com

THE CRAFT BREWERY
THAT HAS TAKEN ROOT
IN THE CITY OF HEINEKEN

Since it was founded in the mid-1980s, this craft brewery has managed to introduce its Flink (lager), IjWit (white), IPA and Zatte (Tripel) into almost every bar in the city.

But the best way to discover the classics and limited editions of Brouwerij 't IJ is to go straight to the source: the former public baths in the shadow of the Gooyer windmill, which have been converted into a tasting room.

BROUWERIJ 'T IJ
FUNENKADE 7

+31 (0)20 261 9801

info@brouwerijhetij.nl
brouwerijhetij.nl

© BROUWERIJ 'T IJ

– **WOUTER TROELSTRA** –

WOUTER HAS BEEN MAKING THE ROUNDS OF THE BARS AND RESTAURANTS
IN AMSTERDAM SINCE 2010 TO PROMOTE BROUWERIJ 'T IJ BEERS.

What sets
the IJ brewery apart?

Established in 1985, it was the very first craft brewery in Amsterdam, at a time when only lagers were brewed here. There are almost fifty breweries today, compared to ten years ago, when there were only nine. Times have definitely changed. What's special about us is that we have our own yeast, which is used in most of our recipes and gives them their unique character. During fermentation, our yeast produces fruity aromas, which make our beers easy to drink. It's very important to us that our beers be balanced and not too extreme.

What makes Amsterdam's craft beer scene so vibrant?

Speciality beers started to become popular in Holland in the early 2010s and the number of breweries has increased exponentially in just a few years.

There's no other city in the Netherlands with so many restaurants and bars – this creates many opportunities for the city's microbreweries and adds to the liveliness of the local beer scene.

How would you define Amsterdam in a few words?

Open, free-spirited, direct and multicultural – and don't forget our love of bikes.

What are your favourite places in Amsterdam to go for a beer?

If it's nice out, you'll find me sipping a Biri at Waterkant (on the Singel) or an IJwit at Café Fonteyn in the centre. And, if it's raining, I'll probably be at Café de Tuin in the Jordaan, with a Zatte in my hand.

© BROUWERIJ T IJ

THE MUMS'
RESTAURANT

Traditional Dutch cuisine may not be the most famous in the world, but if there's one place to try it, it's under the family photos that line the walls at Moeders ('the mums' in Dutch). (You can bring your own photo to round off the collection.) Here, you can try *stamppot* (cabbage and potato purée), *suddervlees* (beef stew) and *erwtensoep* (pea soup) or simply opt for the Dutch *rijsttafel*, an assortment of local specialities inspired by the Indonesian tradition of 'rice tables'.

Don't be surprised by the totally mismatched cutlery – it's what the guests brought with them to the restaurant's opening in 1990.

MOEDERS
ROZENGRACHT 251

moeders.com/en

PARK SOMERLUST, KORTE OUDERKERKERDIJK 16	**MARINETERREIN KATTENBURGERSTRAAT 5**	**ZUIDERBAD HOBBEMASTRAAT 26**
	marineterrein.nl	amsterdam.nl/zuiderbad

WHERE THE DUTCH
GO FOR A DIP

We don't recommend swimming in the narrow canals in the city centre – and not only because of the large numbers of boats (sightseeing and other) and occasional barges. But obviously we totally understand that all this water can make you want to jump into the canals when the weather's nice ...

So if you want to go for a dip, or even practise your breaststroke, do as the Dutch do: head away from the centre and put your towel down along the Amstel, where the canal gets wider. Another option is the inner harbour of the Marineterrein, a military site across from the Nemo Museum, where diving boards and swimming lanes have been specially set up.

And if it's too cold outside, you can always take refuge in the Zuiderbad swimming pool in the museum district. With its ceiling flooded with natural light, period cabins and majestic fountain at the end of the large pool, it will plunge you into the atmosphere of the early 20th century, when this former cycling school was transformed into a pool.

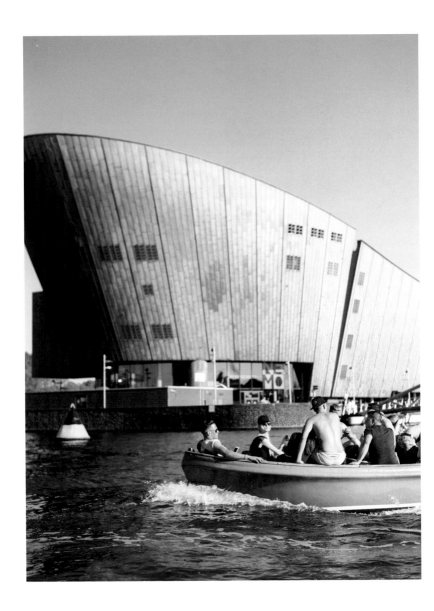

#09

THE MOST
POPULAR MARKET

Albert Cuypmarkt, in the heart of the trendy De Pijp district, or Bloemenmarkt, the flower market along the Singel? Too touristy. The market you shouldn't miss is Dappermarkt, between Mauritskade and Wijttenbachstraat – less central, but much more popular and varied.

The 250 vendors at Dappermarkt, located in Amsterdam's most multicultural area, sell cheese, bread, vegetables, clothes, flowers, accessories and street food from all over the world every day except Sunday.

DAPPERMARKT
DAPPERSTRAAT

dappermarkt.nl

WHAT SHOULD YOU BUY
IN DUTCH MARKETS?

POFFERTJES: typical Dutch-market fare, these fluffy little pancakes are made from yeast and buckwheat flour.

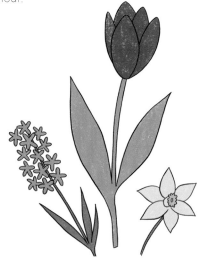

FLOWERS AND BULBS: the Netherlands is one of the world's leading producers of tulips, hyacinths and daffodils, all of which are grown for their bulbs, which are easy to transport across the globe.

STREET FOOD: if you need a break from chips and *bitterballen*, Amsterdam's markets are the ideal place to try specialities from Indonesia and Surinam (two former Dutch colonies) as well as from Vietnam and the Middle East.

STROOPWAFELS:
se 'syrup waffles' are composed of two
in layers of waffle filled with caramel
syrup. Best eaten hot.

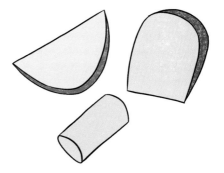

CHEESES: Holland is obviously known for its edam and different varieties of gouda ... but other hard cheeses are also worth a try, including *geitenkaas*, a goat cheese, and Delfts Blauw, a blue cheese from the region of Delft.

SLEEP IN A FORMER
DRAWBRIDGE KEEPER'S CABIN

Over the years, the former drawbridge keepers' cabins along the canals have been turned into 'pocket hotels', sometimes literally suspended over the water.

Each room is unique: some are in the heart of vibrant neighbourhoods while others offer breathtaking views over peaceful expanses of water … And there's something for every budget: from €120 a night to over €1,000 for Amstelschutsluis, a national monument in the middle of the Amstel, accessible only by boat.

📍 **SWEETSHOTEL**

+31 (0)20 740 1010

sweetshotel.amsterdam
post@sweetshotel.amsterdam

© SWEETS HOTEL / MIRJAM BLEEKER & LOTTE HOLTERMAN

THE RESTAURANT
OF DE PIJP REGULARS

Olive & Cookie has just one table and dozens of colourful, seasonal and vegetarian dishes – sometimes original, always delicious. You'll want to try everything, and you can do so because the dishes are sold by weight. When you sit down at the only table, you can be sure that regulars of the De Pijp district will stop by to sample Sandra and Peter's cooking and take it home with them.

N.B: the restaurant closes in the evening once everything prepared that morning has sold out.

OLIVE & COOKIE
SAENREDAMSTRAAT 67

oliveandcookie.com

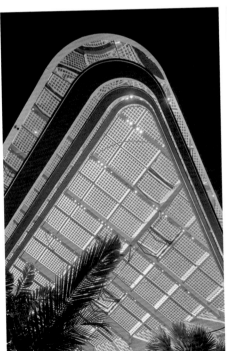

A CRUISE SHIP TERMINAL
REVAMPED
AS A GREEN HOTEL

From 1910 to 1970, Java-eiland was the departure point for ocean liners destined for Indonesia (or rather the 'Dutch East Indies', as it was known until 1949). Today, the peninsula has been transformed into a luxury hotel – a *green* luxury hotel; in fact, with its wooden structure and eco-design, Hotel Jakarta promotes itself as the greenest hotel in town. Its Indonesian-inspired rooms, top-floor cocktail bar and expansive windows overlooking the IJ river provide the perfect backdrop for dreaming of far-flung horizons. The highlight? The majestic indoor garden, with banana trees, several-metre-tall palm trees and tropical flora, which you can explore from a wooden walkway.

 HOTEL JAKARTA AMSTERDAM
JAVAKADE 766

+31 (0)20 236 0000

hoteljakarta.com

© HOTEL JAKARTA

13

THEATRE OF FISH

AN EXTRAVAGANZA CELEBRATING
THE GLORY OF FISH

Just like at a fish market, at Pesca there's no menu: you choose your octopus, swordfish or sea bream from the stall. The evening is punctuated by the sound of a bell announcing a drop in price to sell off stocks. Your dinner is then prepared in the large open kitchen – or directly at your table if it's grilled sardines. Now all that's left is to choose a wine to go with the dish (guided by the sommelier) ... and enjoy the show.

 PESCA
ROZENGRACHT 133

pesca.restaurant

© PESCA

DISCOVER THE AMSTERDAM FOREST
ON A HISTORIC TRAM

Who knew Amsterdam was home to one of the largest urban forests in Europe? Three times the size of New York's Central Park, Amsterdamse Bos can be explored by bike, of course. But the best way to discover it is on the historic tram line 30, which winds 7 km from Haarlemmermeer station to the forest (and back) every Sunday from Easter to October. Themed tours are also offered throughout the year, such as on St Nicholas Day.

📍 **HAARLEMMERMEER STATION**

Easter to October, every SUN; departures every 30 mins

museumtramlijn.org/EN/tramrides.php

DINE IN
A GREENHOUSE

You'll immediately recognise the famous restaurant De Kas, nestled in the heart of Frankendael Park in the east of the city, by its large greenhouse. This is not just a decorative element: the vegetables that comprise the meals served in the restaurant are grown here and in the adjoining garden (supplemented by an organic farm north of Amsterdam). The promise is simple: what you see on your plate was picked that very same morning. It doesn't get much fresher than that!

DE KAS
KAMERLINGH ONNESLAAN 3

+31 (0)20 462 4562

info@restaurantdekas.nl
restaurantdekas.com

© HOTZE EISMA

67

THE RESPONSIBLE
COFFEE ROASTER

The Netherlands has held a special place in the global coffee market since the 16th century: Dutch settlers developed coffee cultivation in Indonesia and Surinam before the country became an import centre. Today, a new wave of roasters is revitalising the craft – like Menno, for example, who created Bocca following a trip to Ethiopia. His credo is fair trade coffee and he sticks to it, from plantation to cup. Try it at his café in Kerkstraat.

BOCCA
KERKSTRAAT 96

info@bocca.nl
bocca.nl

THE RESTAURANT THAT
TRANSPORTS YOU
TO INDONESIA

Indonesian immigrants brought their recipes and the tradition of the 'rice table' (*rijsttafel* in Dutch) – a veritable feast of dishes and flavours – with them to Amsterdam. At Blauw's, this traditional menu includes up to 16 different dishes for sharing, all equally delicious. *Udang goreng* (spicy prawns), *gado gado* (vegetable salad), tempeh with *sambal* sauce, *sate ayam* (chicken skewers), *pisang goreng* (plantains) ... Each small dish is a journey on its own.

BLAUW
AMSTELVEENSEWEG 158-160

restaurantblauw.nl

THE FORMER
SHIPYARD TURNED
TRENDY NEIGHBOURHOOD

On the eve of the Second World War, NDSM was the largest shipyard in the world, a distinction it maintained until the 1960s, when it gradually began to decline.

Today, this former industrial wasteland, which can be reached within minutes by ferry from Amsterdam Central Station, has become a fast-changing, dynamic area encompassing real-estate projects, restaurants, cafés and artists' studios.

NDSM-WHARF

Ferries leave from Amsterdam Central Station every 15 minutes during peak hours and every 30 minutes during off-peak hours. Last departure on SAT and SUN at 3am

ndsm.nl

Van Dijk
and Ko

Ij Kantine

Straat
museum

Ij Hallen

Ljver

Faralda

De Ceuvel

73

PLLEK

STRAAT MUSEUM

VAN DIJK AND KO

IJVER

📍 **PLLEK**
NEVERITAWEG 59

For a drink with your feet
in the sand

pllek.nl

📍 **STRAAT MUSEUM**
NDSM-PLEIN 1

The museum of street art

straatmuseum.com/en

📍 **VAN DIJK AND KO**
PAPAVERWEG 46

2500 m² of warehouses
for bargain hunters

vandijkenko.nl

📍 **IJVER**
SCHEEPSBOUWKADE 72

To try one of
their 30 draught beers

ijveramsterdam.nl

📍 **DE CEUVEL**
KORTE PAPAVERWEG 4

For a coffee at the water's edge

deceuvel.nl

DE CEUVEL

TAKE A BREAK AMONG
THE BONSAI TREES

The designers of the Japanese company Time & Style have made their mark in a former police barracks in the Jordaan: on five floors, furniture, lamps, ceramics and unique objects immerse you in the Japanese art of living ... But the building's best-kept secret is its bonsai garden with a terrace overlooking the canal.

 SHOP TIME & STYLE
MARNIXSTRAAT 148

+31 (0)20 210 3176   timeandstyle.com/amsterdam

継
承
と
創
造

Rund　Bouillabaisse　Thom-Kah-Kai　Spinazie-Oude Kaas　Truffel

THE CITY'S
BEST *BITTERBALLEN*

Kroketten and *bitterballen* – a mixture of breadcrumbs, meat, stock, butter and flour – are staples in all Dutch bars, pairing perfectly with an aperitif. The only difference between the two is their shape: *bitterballen* are round and the croquettes are oblong. To try the traditional version, head over to the counter at Van Dobben. For a more modern approach, the place to go is Ballenbar, opened by Michelin-starred chef Peter Gast and his former sous-chef, Jeroen Elijzen, in the heart of FoodHallen: they have updated the genre with vegan, truffle, bouillabaisse and green curry versions.

VAN DOBBEN
KORTE REGULIERSDWARSSTRAAT 5-7-9

DE BALLENBAR
FOODHALLEN -
HANNIE DANKBAARPASSAGE 16

eetsalonvandobben.nl

deballenbar.com

ART, SCIENCE
AND GASTRONOMY

Art meets science at Mediamatic, an atypical space that opened in 2015 a few steps from Amsterdam Central Station. With the help of its neighbour Hannekes Boom, a bar that's overrun as soon as the weather turns nice, Mediamatic has breathed new life into this neighbourhood, which for years was a no man's land.

In addition to exhibitions and experiments by its artists in residence, the space also features Mediamatic Eten, a restaurant with surprising menus (often with ingredients produced on site), which you can enjoy in one of the detached greenhouses set up along the canal.

📍 **MEDIAMATIC BIOTOOP DIJKSPARK**
DIJKSPARK 6

Guided tour of the premises every
Friday

mediamatic.net

© MEDIAMATIK

 # 22

BROWN CAFÉ
OR WHITE CAFÉ?

There are two types of cafés where you can take a break during the day: the traditional *bruin* (brown) cafés and the white cafés. With their timeworn dark wooden walls, the former are unmissable historical havens. In contrast, the white cafés are much sleeker and brighter, and much less typical of Amsterdam.

> ## CAFÉ HOPPE

Cafe Hoppe, in the heart of the city next to the Begijnhof, is one of Amsterdam's oldest cafés: with its large wooden counter, old paintings and panelling, it is the epitome of a brown café.

CAFÉ HOPPE
SPUI 18-20

+31 (0)20 420 4420   cafehoppe.com

> CAFÉ DE JAREN

Just a few hundred metres away, the white Cafe De Jaren impresses with its light-flooded glass walls and terrace on stilts over the Amstel.

 CAFÉ DE JAREN
NEW DOELENSTRAAT 20

+31 (0)20 625 5771

cafedejaren.nl

OTHER BROWN CAFÉS ...

Café Chris, one of the oldest
Bloemstraat 42
+31 (0)20 624 5942 – cafechris.nl

Café De Tuin, the most spacious
Tweede Tuindwarsstraat 13
+31 (0)20 624 4559

De Pels, the most intellectual
Huidenstraat 25
+31 (0)20 622 9037 – cafedepels.nl

Café T'Mandje, the most LGTB-friendly
Zeedijk 63
cafetmandje.amsterdam

JONGE JENEVER......HOPPE

CAFÉ HOPPE

AN AFTERNOON
DOWN ON THE FARM

Watching sheep graze while you eat your *broodje* (the traditional Dutch sandwich) and sip your Elderberry Bionade, it's hard to believe you're still in the middle of a bustling capital. And yet, just 15 minutes by bike from Amsterdam Central Station, Westerpark is home to a peaceful farm ... You can stop there for a bite to eat and recharge your batteries before taking the ferry to NDSM (at Pontsteiger) or visiting Het Schip, a museum dedicated to the architecture of the Amsterdam School. Or linger longer to enjoy the simple, rural atmosphere and treat yourself to a yoga class.

 BUURTBOERDERIJ 'ONS GENOEGEN'
SPAARNDAMMERDIJK 319

+33 (0)20 337 6820

buurtboerderij.nl
info@buurtboerderij.nl

THE MUST-TRY
RESTAURANT IN DE PIJP

A kimchi muffin? Roasted peach with chickpeas? Broccoli sprout tempura? Ricotta gnudi? A bacon cocktail? The options change often but there's always something surprising on the menu at Little Collins. With a terrace that's perpetually packed on sunny days, this restaurant in the De Pijp district is a must for sharing dishes with unusual flavours for brunch or dinner.

N.B: reservations recommended.

LITTLE COLLINS
EERSTE SWEELINCKSTRAAT 19F

+31 (0)20 753 9636

littlecollins.nl

WATCH A FILM
IN A MYTHICAL THEATRE

When it opened in 1921, the Theater Tuschinski shocked Amsterdammers with its mixture of genres. Influenced by Art Deco, Art Nouveau and the Amsterdam School, its architect created an out-of-the-ordinary building just a stone's throw from Rembrandtplein.

Since then, the cinema has been fully embraced by the city's residents and renovated several times. Today, it serves as a majestic setting for film premieres in the country. Watch a Hollywood blockbuster in the large auditorium, with its chandeliers and period organ, or simply stroll into the lobby to admire the décor and check out the monumental carpet, flown in from Morocco in one piece.

 THEATER TUSCHINSKI
REGULIERSBREESTRAAT 26-34

pathe.nl/bioscoop/tuschinski

© VAN MOOF

– TACO CARLIER –
FOUNDER OF VANMOOF

IN 2009, TACO AND HIS BROTHER FOUNDED THE VANMOOF BIKE BRAND
IN AMSTERDAM. THEIR AMBITION WAS TO DESIGN THE PERFECT CITY BIKE,
WITH ELECTRICAL ASSISTANCE. TODAY,
THEIR MODELS ARE BEING ADOPTED ALL OVER THE WORLD.

Why is cycling so popular in the Netherlands?

The country has the perfect conditions for cycling: it's flat, its cities are small and the climate is good for biking. The good news is that, thanks to electric bikes, other countries can now enjoy these ideal conditions as well …

What sets your bikes apart from others?

Our objective is to make electric bikes the default mode of transportation in cities. We've rethought everything from the bike's design to how it is ridden. Contrary to what is usually the case, we do everything in-house, from A to Z.

How did this idea come about?
It all started in New York, not in Amsterdam. My brother Ties and I were on a business trip. We rented bikes and discovered just how nice it was to cycle there. And yet, surprisingly, there were very few cyclists … That's when we decided to combine Dutch cycling expertise with the latest technology to create VanMoof.

Cycling in Amsterdam for the first time can be stressful for someone who isn't used to it. **Do you have any survival tips?** Stay cool. Don't rush. And everything will be fine!

What are your favourite places to ride a bike in Amsterdam? Along the canals, of course, and especially at night when everything's quiet. Cycling along the Amstel is also brilliant. For a day trip, I recommend cycling to Marken along Lake IJssel (IJsselmeer in Dutch) or to the beach, via Haarlem and then the dunes.

© VAN MOOF

LEARN
EVERYTHING ABOUT
AMSTERDAM'S CANALS

How is the water level in the canals determined? Why is it said that Amsterdam was built on a forest? How are the city's 75 km of canals maintained?

To find the answers to all these questions, head over to Het Grachtenhuis, the 'canal house', a 17th-century mansion along the Herengracht. Here, an immersive presentation and numerous models retrace the history of the city and its canals. Make sure to check out the interior garden before you leave!

HET GRACHTENHUIS
HERENGRACHT 386

grachten.museum/en

BRUNCH IN THE
GARDEN OF THE HERMITAGE

The small garden behind the Hermitage Museum is home to the Hoftuin restaurant, run by the social enterprise Dignita.

After visiting the museum or the nearby Botanical Garden, treat yourself to one of Hoftuin's famous cakes: carrot cake, apple pie, hazelnut and pear bars, coffee brownies ... Not to mention (among other things) mango pancakes marinated in cinnamon and aniseed.

DIGNITA HOFTUIN
NIEUWE HERENGRACHT 18A

eatwelldogood.nl/en/dignita-hoftuin

© DIGNITA

# #
28

THE UNCLASSIFIABLE
HOTEL

Hotel? Flats where you can put down your bags for a night or a month? Shared workspace? Healthy café? Zoku is a bit of all of the above and is on a mission to shake up the hotel world with its hybrid concept, which doesn't fit any box. You don't have to spend a night there to enjoy its charms: the rooftop terrace with greenhouses is open to all, for breakfast, coffee or dinner with a view.

 ZOKU
WEESPERSTRAAT 105

livezoku.com

EXPLORE THE CITY
BY STAND-UP PADDLE

Weather permitting, Morene Dekker and her team offer stand-up paddling tours of the city for all levels.

Beginners can take a course to learn the basics, while the more experienced can go on a two-hour tour, from Zeeburg to the city centre on Thursday evening or from IJburg beach to Muiden Castle on Thursday morning.

On Wednesday and Sunday mornings, you can even take a yoga class on a board out on the water.

© MM SUP

 MM SUP
IJBURG BEACH (PAMPUSLAAN 500)
AND ZEEBURGERPAD 10

mm-sup.com

AN UNFORGETTABLE MEAL
ON A TIMELESS ISLAND

Vuurtoreneiland ('Lighthouse Island') is a small island about 10 km from the centre of Amsterdam, accessible only by boat … And the only way to get there is to book a table at the restaurant that has taken refuge there. Allow plenty of time – about five hours – for a unique adventure.

In winter, you'll be served by the fire in the old fort designed to protect Amsterdam from Prussian attacks; in summer, in a large greenhouse facing the water, surrounded by nature.

The five-course menu is designed around local and seasonal vegetables, complemented by meat and fish, all slow-cooked over a wood fire.

 VUURTORENEILAND
DEPARTURES FROM IN FRONT OF THE LLOYD HOTEL,
OOSTELIJKE HANDELSKADE 34

Reservations open two months in advance.
Afternoon boat trip with guided tour every third FRI of the month (without lunch or dinner at the restaurant)

vuurtoreneiland.nl

we never reveal the 31st address in the 'Soul of' series
because it's strictly confidential.
Up to you to find it!

THE SECRET BUNKER
IN THE VONDELPARK

Amsterdam's most central park is home to a vestige from the war: a bunker, which, in the tradition of the self-managed venues that have flourished in Amsterdam since the 1960s, is occupied by a collective that regularly organises electro evenings, screenings, exhibitions and concerts there ... But we've already given too much away: now it's up to you to find the front door.

 STARTING POINT:
VONDELPARK

Look for the Vondelpark fallout shelter ... or its website, where you'll find the venue's programme

---

love is an art
Art is a choice
Choice is freedom
Freedom is an expression
Vondelbunker
is an expression of love

MANY THANKS TO

FANY for her friendship, curiosity and enthusiasm.

CAMILLE for giving me the opportunity to discover the soul of Amsterdam.

MAUD, RENZO, MANU, GUI, SAMI, BABAK AND STEVEN for welcoming me in what is now their city.

NATHALIE, CLÉMENCE, EMMANUELLE, PAULINE AND PHILIPPINE for their invaluable assistance.

THOMAS, expedition leader.

This book was created by:
Benoit Zante, texts
Pauline Walzak, photos
Philippine Lugol, illustrations
Emmanuelle Willard Toulemonde, layout
Sophie Schlondorff, translation
Jana Gough, editing
Kimberly Bess, proofreading
Clémence Mathé, publishing

You can write to us at contact@soul-of-cities.com
Follow us on Instagram on @soul_of_guides

THANK YOU

In the same collection:

Soul of Athens
Soul of Barcelona
Soul of Berlin
Soul of Kyoto
Soul of Lisbon
Soul of Los Angeles
Soul of Marrakesh
Soul of New York
Soul of Rome
Soul of Tokyo
Soul of Venice

© JONGLEZ 2023
Registration of copyright: April 2023 – Edition: 01
ISBN: 978-2-36195-466-6
Printed in Slovakia by Polygraf